Coming Together

By Art Gibson

Chapter One

"Hey, Toby. You want to go to the Oilers' game with me? My dad's got an extra ticket for tonight's game."

Woody and I always tried to attend a Tulsa Oilers hockey game. Scoring a free ticket was boss. Going with my best friend made my insides quiver.

I wanted to go with him so badly I could taste it. Woody and I had been friends since pre-kindergarten. We played all the kid games growing up. His parents and my dad thought of us as brothers from different mothers.

Somehow, we developed a love of the game of hockey, somewhat unusual for two kids from a non-hockey state like Oklahoma.

"Not tonight, Woody. I need to get home."

"The game is gonna be a good one."

He finished speaking and stared at my face, looking for what he always saw on it. I knew he was looking for the makeup I usually wore. Today, I had chosen to forego any makeup.

"What's the deal, Toby? Not wearing makeup. You always wear makeup. It makes you look special."

Woody knew my makeup expressed my feelings of freedom from a society that dictated what was appropriate for the gender-identity of the individual. That society held prejudice against a boy who doesn't conform by doing what was considered appropriate for a girl..

If wearing makeup made them think of me as a girl, they were wrong. I definitely was not girly. I was all boy. Except, I liked to wear makeup. It was like saying to society, *Stick it!*

My best friend was okay with my wearing makeup, standing up against the bullies when they tried to hassle me. Once he had told me it made me look desirable.

Trying to clear his confusion, I said. "My dad hadn't gone to work when I was getting ready. I can't let him see me wearing makeup."

Aiden, my younger brother, standing beside us, growled. "Our dad's suspicious of us all the time. He goes to that bar on the corner. He meets Dirk and his empty brained brother. They fill him with anti-gay hogwash. He comes home and rants at us. He needs to give it a break."

Aiden and I were close, as much as the two years that separated us allowed. He always tagged along with us, even eating lunch with us at school. Some of our friends thought it weird that Woody and I were close and we let Aiden hang with us.

"Those losers have tried to convince Woody that you are a gay boy trying to turn him, recruit him so you can have your way with him." Aiden spat.

Woody said with kindness. "Toby's my best friend. You know that Aiden. I'll be who I am and like who I like."

Yeah, Woody was my best friend next to my brother. Aiden, my fifteen-year-old brother, knew about me wearing makeup and why I wore it. Once he let me fix his face with everything, including lipstick. I saw him smile when he looked in the mirror, taking different poses as he studied his face.

"I like it, especially the eyeliner. It accents my eyes and I see a different me. I understand why you wear it."

I cleaned his face when he finished. He was beautiful in a boyish way and the makeup accented his features. After he was makeup free, He hugged me, thanking me and kissed my cheek.

Yeah, I wanted to protect Aiden from our dad. I was worried. The stuff dad might do to me or have done to me made my insides quake. Protecting Aiden could be difficult. I was a seventeen-year-old skinny dude with a few undeveloped muscles trying to keep my brother safe.

Aiden continued. "Dad hates gays. He rants about them destroying our society. If he discovers you wear makeup…."

His voice trailed off, a scared look on his face.

Woody, ever ready to help, came to the rescue.

"You guys can crash at my place if it comes to that. We have an extra room. My 'rents are cool. They are buying a Pride flag to support LGBTQ kids and adults. They started attending PFLAG meetings. I might be Pan. I haven't figured myself out. Sometimes I think the 'rents would like me to be totally gay so they can throw a coming out party. I mean, I'm okay with kids who identify as a different gender than that assigned at birth. They're kids trying to figure things out. Why should I hate them?"

Then he turned to me.

"If I were to have a gay boyfriend, I'd want you to be that boy. I may have feelings for you. If trouble comes your way, I stand with you."

"I'll help you, Toby. You're the best
'her."

A tear dripped from my eye. I had
'the best friends a boy could want.
"hanks."

ɔked at my little brother. At
ɩegan a growth spurt a year ago.
ɩg.   ɬ four inches above me, though
ɔ"   ɩed him.

ʰᵉ   ﹐ighteen next month and be
                ɪraduate, watch how fast I

ɔnal if
ɇ gay."   ˡept my mouth shut
ɔody's.   ɬen's face fell. He
                ɪy words. I knew

ɬasses.
ɬd ditch   I'll stick around
ɇve my   ɩoth move out
ɔut. Aiden   to smooth

ɬered. "Dad.   ɩ us until
                ˡer's

"If you change your mind, I still got the tickets."

"Thanks, Woody. But we better get home after school."

Aiden and I walked out of the lunchroom, talking low.

"Listen Toby, dad was acting weird this morning. I think he suspects somethir We may have trouble when we get home

My heart jumped. "Shit! What if l discovers my makeup?"

"If he does, you're gonna be in a world of hurt, Toby. Dad can be irrati he suspects you, or even me, might b

"We'll move the makeup to W Dad won't find it at his house."

We headed for our separate All afternoon, I wondered if I shou my classes, sneak home, and retri makeup. In the end, I toughed it and I arrived home together.

As we entered, Aiden ho We're home."

I breathed a sigh of relief as the silence enveloped us. I ran to where I hid my stuff, reaching into the back of my closet, feeling for my winter boots where I hid my supplies.

For an emergency, I kept some money with my makeup. A wadded up sock on top of it all helped create an illusion of carelessness. I pulled the boot out. No sock, makeup, or money. My heart thumped.

"Aiden" I called. My weak voice cracking.

My brother came to stand by the closet. He saw me holding the empty boot.

His fist went to his mouth. "Oh, shit." He knew what that missing makeup signified.

"Dad found it. He found my stash. What am I going to do? Dad will kill me. This will convince him I am gay. I gotta get out of here before he comes home."

I dumped my books from my backpack to stuff whatever clothes I might need inside of it. My stomach burned. I finished making ready and turned to Aiden.

"Gotta go. I love you, Bro. I'll come get you when I find a place."

I held him tightly, not wanting to let him go.

"If dad gets rough, run to Woody's."

Aiden had tears in his eyes. He followed me down the stairs. I took one last look around. I went to the kitchen and grabbed a couple of power bars, then turned for the front door.

"Going somewhere, queer boy?"

Dad stood blocking the doorway. My makeup bag dangled by his fingertips as if he was afraid he might catch something from holding it.

I blustered. "That stuff is mine. Give it to me. I want my money too."

"Well, well. Not holding this makeup for your girlfriend? Oh, that money belongs to me. You won't need it where you're going."

Dad's face had a deep red blush to it, like he got when he became furious.

He was big. I'll give him that. His body was not muscle. He was flabby. Flab that developed from sitting at the bar, guzzling beer, and spewing anti-gay nonsense.

I turned, hoping to run out the backdoor. I saw a hulking brute of a man dressed in black, barring that exit. Dirk blocked my way. I looked at the kitchen window. Dirk raised his index finger in a motion that warned me not to attempt that way out.

I turned back to look at a man, who, in this moment, ceased to be a father to me.

"This junk yours, or is it your brothers?"

My defeated look was admission enough for dad.

"Do you know what we do to queers?"

"Don't call me that." I spat at him.

Dad went on as if I had not spoken.

"Dirk and AI know how to change your kind. They ~~them~~ <ins>turn</ins> them straight."

Dad grinned evilly, then nodded at Dirk, before returning his face to me.

"When you return, you won't be a queer. These men are going to cure you. They assured me their methods will change you and cure you forever." <ins>a feel of</ins>

I felt a cold tightness in my gut. I ~~felt~~ helpless, trapped. ~~So~~ I blurted. <ins>My Anger</ins>

"I'll never return to you, ever. I <ins>shall</ins> <ins>out</ins> disown you."

"We'll see about that. Strip him."

I fought. These huge goons overpowered me, ripping my clothes from me, until I stood naked in front of the man I used to call dad. Him seeing me naked was beyond embarrassing. I tried to cover my private area. ~~I shivered~~ <ins>shivered and</ins>.

Aiden could see all that was going on. I felt more ashamed of Aiden seeing me than my dad seeing me. I looked at my brother. He refused to look at my naked body, holding his hands over his eyes.

A trapped, helpless feeling

I felt a prick in my neck. The world went black.

I awoke, my mouth felt as if it was full of cotton. My eyes could not make out my surroundings.

"Water. I need water." I moaned into a darkened room. No answer. "Water, please."

Still nothing. I heard the rumbling of my stomach. When had I last eaten?

I shivered with fear and felt cold. I patted for my clothes. I was naked. *They were missing.*

I cried, hoping this was all a dream, yet knowing it was real.

I remembered Aiden, alone with the monster I used to think of as a dad. What was this evil man doing to Aiden?

I needed to get to him. Protect him. I hoped even now he was not being abused.

Laying on a floor in the dark, I could not gauge the passing of time. I sat up when the door opened. I felt the coolness of the breeze from the hallway passing over my skin.

"You are awake. Good."

"Where am I? Could you get me some water and some food? Please?"

"You are in no position to demand anything. It's time for your first therapy. Get up."

He arms around me forced me to stand. I tried to hold my body limp. He overpowered me, laughing as he lifted me.

"What therapy?" I asked

He laughed more.

The dim light of the hall showed Dirk walking ahead of me. I had a rope around my waist. Whenever I tried to hold back, he pulled on it. I had no choice. I felt so embarrassed walking without my clothes. He led me into a room. In the center stood a table like you might find in a hospital operating room, the kind I had seen on TV hospital shows. Al stood at the head of the table.

"Let's get him tied." He said to Dirk.

I wiggled and screamed. They ignored my protests, tying my hands and feet, spreading me. I had no feelings of privacy as I lay exposed to their stares.

"Can you cover me, at least?"

I wanted something to cover my nakedness, to hide me from their leering looks. I felt shame and humiliation at them seeing me like this.

Al spoke with an edge to his voice. I smelled alcohol on his breath. His eyes had a sheen to them as he licked his lips. I tried to squirm away from his looks, from the way he seemed to derive pleasure from my discomfort.

"Your type likes to flaunt yourselves. So we are letting you do it. When we finish with your treatment, you will be childlike and won't feel emotions. And forget about doing what boys so much enjoy. You will no longer have the desire or ability."

I felt a chill deep inside. I wanted to cry. They did not deserve my tears. I needed my energy to plot my escape.

"When is that doctor coming?" Dirk asked.

"Tomorrow. He needs to get the anesthetic to perform that lobo procedure."

"You don't even know how to say that word, you jerk. It's called a lobotomy."

The two continued talking. If I had been scared before, I was in a panic now. I knew about the effects of a lobotomy from my Psych class.

They would cut some nerves in my brain, making me lose the ability to experience intense emotions. I would revert to childish behavior. I would never become a fully functioning adult. Mentally, I would be a boy in an adult's body.

"No!" I screamed until my throat hurt.

"Go ahead, gay boy. Practice how to scream for what's coming."

Al seemed to enjoy telling me this. I felt Dirk grab my penis. "He'll need to be hard for what's next. You said you are thirsty. Have a drink."

He had to make me drink, holding my nose so I swallowed. They left the room for a while. When they returned, Dirk said. "I think that's enough time.

"Rub him." Al said.

"I ain't rubbing his cock. That's gay."

"We are being paid enough. Wear those latex gloves. You can rub this kid's penis and get him hard for the money we are getting."

I tried to ignore what Dirk was doing to me as his hand stroked me in the way I knew would achieve his final goal. I felt myself responding and tried to picture dead puppies. No use. I was exposed and on display. ~~I cried~~.

"Please. Don't do this. I will be a good boy."

Of course, they ignored me.

"The kid's got a good one. Too bad we got to ruin it. I bet you masturbate often. Right kid? After you leave here, touching yourself to pee will hurt. You may have to sit like a girl to pee."

Al laughed and said. "He uses makeup. Maybe he fancies himself a girl.

That right, kid? You want to be a girl? We could make you one. The doc could cut you. Yeah, take all the parts that show you are a guy."

"Shut up, Al. His dad said nothing about neutering him. I gotta start his treatment."

I felt a sleeve being slid over my now erect penis. I raised my head. Two wires attached to the sides of a sleeve around my penis lead to a box with a dial on top. They plugged the box's wire into a wall socket. Sweat drenched my body.

"Okay, gay boy. See this?" Dirk held a box with the wires attached. "We are going to shock your penis. Burn it so every time you touch the scar tissue on it, you will feel pain. We will do this over the next few days. When we are done, you will barely be able to hold it to pee, much less rub it to get off. That tube you got hanging off you that you like to play with will be a mass of scar tissue."

He took a drink from a bottle, then passed the bottle to his brother.

"We ain't wasting this good liquor on you, gay boy. No anesthetic."

They thought that was funny and laughed.

"Guys, no. Please, don't...."

Dirk cut me off mid-sentence.

"Don't matter. We will burn you and the doc will change you, so you will be nothing, except a little kid."

The next instant, a deep burning pain in my penis caused me to howl. I felt my head thrashing and my body trying to escape its bonds. The deep burning pain never stopped. My tip felt like it was melting. I arched my midsection and froze. Then, nothing.

As if in a far-off distance, I heard voices. "Did we kill him?"

"He's breathing. Damn! We better untie him. He might have a stroke. Look at that fried flesh on his penis. Maybe we went too far for the first time. Doc will check him.

out. I'm going home. You watch him. Go easy on the booze."

I heard a door closing. My dick felt like it was on fire. I gasped at a pain like I had never felt in my life. I sought relief and found none.

I wanted to sink into a deep sleep, but what they told me about tomorrow's procedure sent shivers through my body. Cutting away part of my brain so I would think as a child gave me thoughts of killing myself rather than suffer that fate. My brain sought a solution, a way to get free. I needed to live. I did not want to die at seventeen. I needed to find an escape, even if the attempt killed me.

They had removed the restraints, probably thinking my pain would keep me from leaving. I struggled to sit on the edge of the bed. I wanted to scream at the intense pain every movement caused. My vision darkened. I felt dizzy. Using a great effort, I stood next to the bed. Checking the room for something with which to cover myself, I saw nothing. Escaping without clothes would be better than staying and suffering my fate they planned.

Shuffling to the door. I tried the knob. It turned. Trying not to let the door squeak, I opened the door enough to peer into the hall. To my right were more doors, probably bedrooms. To my left, I made out the flickering of a TV. I shuffled in that direction, each step bringing me intense pain. At the end of the hall, I made out Al in a chair. His mouth hung open; a whiskey bottle held in his hand. I looked the other way to see a kitchen area, a door to the outside on the back wall.

The pain intensified. I looked to the refrigerator as a source for ice. But knowing I needed to get away, I focused on the door. Its window revealed the blackness of the night outside. I put my eye to the window, trying to ignore the pain in my groin. The yard looked empty. In the distance, I saw lights. I probably was in a town or a city.

Maybe I could find a cop or someone to help me.

As I opened the door, I heard Al belch. I froze. He resumed snoring. I slipped outside, shutting the door. Rain beat against my skin, causing me to shiver. The coolness of the rainwater gave me some relief from the pain.

I surveyed my surroundings. Next to the door, on the porch, were flip-flops. I put them on. I could walk faster wearing them.

Stepping away from the house, I put my hand into my mouth to keep from screaming. I gritted my teeth, setting off towards a cluster of lights.

The lights scared me. Someone could discover me without clothes. They could capture me.

I approached a gas station focusing on a dumpster. The dumpster reminded me of food that got dumped inside, which reminded me of how empty my stomach felt. I crouched behind the dumpster, hiding my nudity.

Should I walk into the station and tell them someone had kidnapped me and for them to call the cops? Oh. Man, the police would send me back to my dad and then Al and Dirk would retake me and never let me go. They would make me into a mindless child.

Shaking at this thought and the chill rain, I saw a car pull up to the pumps. A tall man, dressed all in black, stepped out and walked to the pump. Maybe I could use his car to escape once he finished. I waited until he went to go into the station to make my move.

My dick throbbed. I ~~ignored~~ *snoring* its pain, ~~putt~~*put*ing my plan into motion.

Crouching low, I scooted for the car's rear door. A flip-flop broke and came off. I kicked off the other.

Reaching the car's door, I considered the interior light that would come on when I opened the door. I looked inside the station. The guy had his back to me as he talked to the clerk. Wasting no further time, I opened the door and threw myself on the back floor, landing on my sore dick. I bit my lip hard, tasting blood.

Laying there, shivering from the cold and the injustice of my situation, I stifled my sobs. My pain intensified as my penis rubbed the carpet. I bit my lip.

The front door opened. The driver flung a package over the back of his seat. I heard it connect with the rear seat. The car started. I was not a praying type, only now I felt the need to pray, like right now. I asked the creator of the universe for a favor.

I felt the car gain speed. We had to be driving on a highway. I lost track of how much time passed. I knew I had to stay awake so that when the car stopped, I could open the door and escape. The car slowed. I could feel it turn, then I felt the bumps of the road we were on. I felt extreme burning as my penis rubbed the carpet. I jammed a fist into my mouth, biting it against the intense pain.

Tears streamed from my eyes at the pain and at my situation. I was almost ready to give myself up to this driver when the car slowed and stopped.

I tried to get up to open the door. My pain doubled. I tried to hide my moan, but it escaped my mouth. ~~I cried harder.~~ *Tear flower aster*

The rear door opened. *Pop* I looked up to stare at the most humongous gun I ever saw pointing at me. I sobbed. All hope fled. My life would end here in the back of some lousy car, with a burned penis. I would never see Aiden again, or Woody. My tears flowed as I shook uncontrollably. I felt I had reached the end of my life.

"Get your ass out of my car."

I could not see beyond the gun with the light blinding me.

"Uh, I have a bit of trouble here. I am cramped, and I am hurt."

"Get out now." I put one hand up, trying to shield my vision from that blinding light.

I struggled, twisting, finally forcing my cramped muscles to work against the intense pain. I clutched the open door to pull myself to stand next to it.

My embarrassment intensified as his light revealed my nakedness, my tears. He had to see the burns. I gave up.

"Shoot me! I can't take the pain. End this pain."

I slumped, praying he would shoot me yet hoping he wouldn't.

"What happened to you? Why are you naked? What's with your penis? It looks like a burned hotdog."

Those words were the last I heard as I felt myself hit the ground. Then blackness.

Chapter Two

I was alive. I felt warm. Not feverish, warm, comfortable warm. The room was bright. I felt the softness of a mattress under me.

"Hey, Gabe. The kid's waking."

I turned to see a young man setting aside a book and walking toward me. I tried to thrash and get away. A soft hand stroked my shoulder.

"Easy there, kid. Nobody here wants to hurt you."

I sensed movement behind the young man, turning my head to see another man in the door opening. A taller version of the guy next to my bed stood in the doorway, staring at me. I moved my hands to hide my junk. I felt cloth. I explored my legs. They were naked. I checked my stomach. I had a shirt covering it.

"Easy kid. You are safe." The man at the door spoke.

I passed out.

I woke later. Someone was touching my penis. I screamed.

"Easy, easy. I have to change your dressing."

The hands touching me were soft. They were placing something on my penis. I screamed as I remembered the sleeve and the burning.

A hand appeared in front of my eyes. It held a piece of gauze with a plastic coating.

"I'm just putting a bandage on your dick, man. You burned it badly. What did you try to do? Roast it like a hot dog?"

I shook my head, though I tried to speak through my aching throat.

"I'm Ralph Ivanov. Gabe's brother. He's the one who found you in his car. Why were you naked, dude? How'd you burn your dick?"

"Shut-up Ralphie. Give the kid a break."

Turning to me, this tall handsome man said. "I'm Gabriel. You can call me Gabe. This other guy is my little brother, Ralph Ivanov."

"He's been taking care of your burn. After he finishes, I'd like you to try getting up and walking."

"How long have I been here?" Why are you being so nice to me?"

"The answer to your first question is that you have been here six days. The answer to your second one is that you needed care. I surmised you did not want the authorities involved, judging by the type and extent of your injuries."

"Thanks." I said nothing else.

I felt better. My penis felt better. I wondered how my brother was doing, and Woody. I decided not to reveal anything else as they might be playing me.

Ralph helped me sit on the bed's edge. I was naked from the waist down. I tried to cover myself.

Sensing my discomfort, the man known as Gabe said.

"We need you uncovered below the waist. You screamed when we tried to cover you. We saw the burns on your raw penis oozing fluid when we got you here. It's scabbing over, finally. Hopefully, there will be new flesh. You may have scar tissue, which will be an issue. I have a plastic surgeon friend who agreed to examine you this evening. She may know how to prevent scarring."

Gabe leaned closer. His eyes concerned and caring.

"What happened that your penis got that way?"

"Yeah dude. We don't even know your name." Ralph said, his tone not threatening.

Looking at these two who had cared for me and protected me, I felt maybe I had found a safe place. I held back my tears and looked from one brother to another. I shuddered, giving up trying to be brave. The tears flowed. I was safe.

I unburdened myself, trusting them. "Thank you. Other than my brother and my best friend Woody, no one ever gave me this kind of care. They certainly never tried to care for my penis. I kinda would like them to care for it, but right now it hurts like a bitch."

Gabe looked at Ralph. "I told you too much pain medicine is not good for someone. Look how he is babbling."

They led me to a room that must have been a dining room, with the big table and the chairs. Ralph carefully eased me into a seat.

He and Gabe joined me at the table.

"Shit. I forgot water." Ralph said, jumping up and returned with a tall glass of water. "The doctor says hydration will help with your healing."

"Why are you so nice? You don't know me. Woody knows me. Aiden loves me. Where is good old Aiden?"

"Drink water to clear your system. Then we talk."

I drank a ton of water. So much I had to pee. Ralph helped me to the toilet and sat me there."

"Can I get some privacy? Then I giggled because they had seen me naked for the past six days as they tended to my injuries. They cleaned and bandaged my

penis for cripes sake. They cleaned me when
I pooped. What hadn't they seen? I shook
my head to shake off my embarrassment.

"Never mind. It's okay, guys. Just
help me back to bed when I am done."

Back in my bed, resting against thick
pillows, I stared at these guys who did not
know me, yet they helped me. I smiled.

"When Gabe and I suffered as teens,
friends and family helped us. This is our
way to pay to repay them. We help you."
Ralph seemed to feel the need to let me
know about his and Gabe's past.

"What do I have to do to repay you?"

"You owe us nothing. The way to
repay us is to do good for others. A French
missionary, Stephen Grellet gave a saying
my brother and I find useful to guide our
lives. 'I shall pass this way but once; any
good that I can do or any kindness that I can
show to any human being, let me do it now,
for I will not pass this way again.' Most
would agree with this yet find it hard to

practice. You can repay us by making this your life's plan."

I sipped more water thinking about what he said. I could start now putting the idea into practice. I studied each of them. They were not the same age, yet they looked like twins. I swallowed more water. Then I started.

"Two days ago, my dad arranged for me to be kidnapped and taken to this house where two men he knew would make sure I would never be gay. They did this to me."

I nodded at my penis, telling them the rest of the story, about the burning and the excruciating pain. I told them how they planned an operation that would change my brain. I withheld nothing from them.

Gabe studied me for the longest time.

"That is beyond belief, almost. If we did not see the results of their sadistic behavior, your story would be hard to believe."

As Gabe finished, the doorbell rang. What happened next blew me away. Gabe reached behind his back. Instantly, an enormous gun appeared in his hand. He nodded at Ralph, who pushed a button on his phone.

Looking at the screen, he announced. "It's the doc."

Ralph moved towards the door. Gabe relaxed, but he continued to hold the gun.

A moment later, a tall woman dressed casually walked into the room. I saw Ralph wave at Gabe. He stuck the gun back into his waistband.

"Welcome Jillie. Glad you came. How's the family? Sam still driving the truck? River and Cale enjoying married life?"

Thanks for asking. I think Sam will retire someday; I hope. River and Cale are adopting a second boy. They love being parents. You need to take a break. Spend some time with my boys and meet little Callie.

"Aw, you know how our work is, always some shit or another going down. How's your practice doing these days?"

"Just fine. I enjoy working under Doctor Kramer. He is a skilled surgeon. I've learned much."

"Thanks for coming on short notice. Let me introduce you to Toby. He's your patient.

I watched this interaction between these people. They talked about people I did not know. The lady doc looked older than I expected a doc should look. She walked to me, holding out her hand. I reached for it and we shook.

"Toby I am Jillie Makin. I'm a nurse practitioner. I'm like a doctor, without the formal finishing training. I specialize in surgery to repair skin defects. Gabe and Ralph are long-time friends of my husband, Sam, and me."

Ralph interrupted. "Jillie knew us when we were teens before she went to medical school."

Jillie added. "I knew them. Both of them were little shits in their teen years. Now? Well, they have grown up physically. That's all I'm going to say. So, what seems to be your issue?"

I froze. This lady, a doctor or nurse practitioner, was not looking at my junk, even if it was burned." *his*

Gabe kneeled next to me. He had a kind presence. He lay a hand on my thigh.

"Jillie's a trained medical professional. You need to show her your injury."

Jillie kneeled on my side opposite Gabe her soft eyes searched my face. "Toby. I am trained in the art of healing. I need your permission to examine you. I have seen boys and men without their clothes. I hope you will trust me to help you."

"But what they did to me. It's too horrible to show you"

I swallowed. Then, with my voice barely above a whisper, I nodded. "Okay."

"Would you let Gabe help you?"

I nodded

Her tone somehow gave me peace. Gabe held my arm as I stood.

Her hands were soft as she carefully removed the dressing.

"Gabe, would you remove Toby's shirt, please?"

With my shirt removed, I shivered. I stood naked in front of the first woman to see me like this since I was an infant and mommy saw me.

Jillie tenderly moved my penis around as she examined it. She did not hurt me. I saw her looking closely at the scabs. I saw the worst burn was on foreskin. *the*

She pushed at parts of my penis, asking me if that caused me pain. Only when she touched my foreskin did I jump.

Finally, she finished her examination.

"Have a seat Toby. We'll re-bandage this in a minute."

Gabe placed a towel over my shoulder. Jillie spoke. "The worst of the burns are on the foreskin. They will cause problems in the future. Your foreskin will be wrinkled and will not heal correctly. You will experience a constant pain in that area. The rest of your penis will grow new skin with minimal scarring. I will give you ointment to help with the healing and help prevent scar tissue from interfering with normal functions."

She was too polite to amplify those normal functions guys enjoy.

"The scar tissue your foreskin will interfere with your ability to urinate and engage in normal male sexual practices. Therefore, I recommend we remove the foreskin."

Seeing me tense, she added. "The procedure takes place using local anesthetic. I inject that into your penis. You will not feel pain. After I remove the foreskin, I use stitches on the remaining edges.

Usually, I only prescribe acetaminophen for pain. Since you have those burns, I will prescribe a stronger drug that you take for two to three days.

"You want to cut me? You are going to take part of my penis?" I could not believe what she suggested.

"It won't hurt with the anesthetic. I perform this procedure routinely."

"On boys my age?"

"Not as often as I perform the procedure on infants, but yes, I have done this procedure on young adults. I believe this is your best option to have a fulfilling life free of pain."

I looked at Gabe. "What do you think?"

"They circumcised Ralph and I as infants. I know it may scare you to be cut at your age. If Jillie recommends doing this, I say follow her recommendation. The good news is you only need this procedure once." He chuckled as he spoke that last sentence.

I rolled my eyes at him. "Smart ass!"

Ralph added, his caring eyes taking in my hesitancy. "We trust Jillie for all our surgical needs. Plus, she is very discrete."

I looked between the three. I liked my foreskin.

As if knowing my thoughts, Jillie said. "After the foreskin is removed, you may find you need a lubrication for your glans. That's your tip that the foreskin covers. Your foreskin protected your glans while you were being burned. You can achieve pleasure as before."

Boy, did I feel myself blush. I never discussed this subject. Not with Woody, and certainly not with my brother.

Ralph smiled. "Of course, you need to heal, not just from the surgery, but from the burns before you do that."

Jillie said. "I will continue to examine you until you are fully healed. I will clear you for sexual activities when I feel you will not hurt yourself."

"How long?"

"That depends on the burns. They should be healed in three weeks, maybe four. That's as long as the circumcision healing will take. I will remove the stitches after about four days."

"Do you think I should do this, Gabe?"

"I do."

I looked into his eyes. They showed his truth and caring for me as well as his trust in Jillie.

"Okay. When do we do we start?"

Jillie took charge, again.

"In the morning. I will bring my kit and we will get this done."

She examined my penis one more time. "I think it will be okay to leave the dressing off tonight. Let him sleep with just a bedsheet over him. He can wear a long, warm shirt. See you tomorrow, Toby."

Ralph escorted Jillie to the door. Again, I noticed Gabe held a gun in his hand.

Gabe must have noticed me watching him hold the gun.

"Toby. In our line of work, we need to take precautions. A moment's lapse in precaution could allow people who want to hurt us to be successful."

"What do you guys do?"

"Well, what we do is not illegal. We help people who need our help, our protection. I will tell you all about our line of work later."

Chapter Three

I woke and stumbled to the toilet. Today I would lose an important part of myself. I felt like my friend was heading for his execution.

I need to quit stressing. Jillie recommended this. Gabe and Ralph, well, I trusted them. They trusted Jillie. I needed to get out of my head and agree with her.

I cursed my dad and those two drunks he called friends. He caused my troubles with his homophobic attitude.

Gabe called from the hall. "Toby? It's almost time. You ready?"

"Yeah. Give me five minutes."

I looked at my reflection. The one person I wanted with me, no the two people who should be here, were Aiden and Woody. I wish I could ask them for advice. I felt so alone.

Leaving my room felt like I was walking my last mile. Not having a covering over my penis. I felt exposed. The heck with it. Everyone had seen me.

A sheet had been placed over the dining room table that covered what appeared to be a foam mattress. This would be where my mutilation happened. Jillie stood at a side table looking at me as I entered.

"I'm ready, if you are." Her face showed confidence. "I covered this table for sterility. We will put a sterile sheet over you. It has an opening where I can expose the operation site.

I wanted to tell her to forget the entire operation. Then I shivered. I felt a strong premonition that something bad was about to happen to my brother, Aiden.

"Wait. Hold on. Aiden, my brother, lives with that fruitcake who used to be my dad. Now that I have escaped, he might turn his attention to Aiden."

Gabe asked for my address, which I gave him. I saw him punch a button on his cell. He spoke, giving whoever answered my address.

"Yes, Priority One. Full assault team and gear. A kiddo might be in danger. His name is Aiden Matthewson."

Disconnecting, he directed his attention to me. I sent a team to your house. They will find Aiden and bring him here where we can care for him. Your dad will not hurt your brother. Now, let's get you fixed up.

I wanted to ask what he meant by a team. I did not have the opportunity. Jillie nodded. Gabe and Ralph helped me to the table.

"Wait. I need to talk to Woody."

"Who's Woody?" Gabe asked. He did not seem frustrated that I was holding up the operation.

"Woody grew up with me. We share everything, even tell each other our most secret thoughts."

Gabe handed me his cell phone. I called Woody. No answer. I left a message telling him to call this number. Dejectedly, I gave the cell to Gabe. I told him that Woody was a friend, a special friend. I told him Woody's address.

Looking with fake sternness at me, he had a grin when he asked. "Anyone else?"

"Naw. Let's do this." I said this with the tone of someone walking to his execution.

Climb on Toby." Jillie said. "Did you take that pill this morning. The one I gave you yesterday."

"I did."

She nodded as they lay me on my back and covered me.

I felt scared and vulnerable, not wanting to watch what she was doing, in case I chickened out. Ralph stood near my head, his hand on my shoulder.

"I will be here at your head, holding your hand. The procedure will not hurt with the anesthetic. Squeeze my hand if you must."

I felt my penis being moved through an opening in the sheet.

Jillie leaned close to my head.

"I will give you an injection that will mask the pain. If you feel any pain, let me know. You should not. Still, let me know. Gabe will assist me with the procedure. Do you have questions?"

I shook my head. "Let's get started."

I clenched my jaw. Ralph held my hand. I felt a tear trickle from my eye and Ralph's hand brush it away.

"It'll be okay. Buddy."

"A tiny prick."

I felt a slight pain at the base of my penis, replaced immediately by a numb feeling.

"You are doing good, buddy."

I felt thankful for Ralph's presence.

"Feel anything?" Jillie's voice asked.

I shook my head, no.

"You will feel some pulling and pressure. That will be all."

I squeezed Ralph's hand while he told me I was doing good. He must have sensed I did not want a blow by blow description, or a cut by cut analysis.

Now and then he brushed my hair and told me I was brave. I continued to feel tugging and pressure."

"There. All done. That was easy. Do you want to see what I removed?"

"God, no. Just get rid of it."

There was more movement around my penis. I felt some pressure and some tugging. They removed the sheet covering me. Ralph helped me sit and swing my legs over the table. He and Gabe guided me over to the couch.

Jillie came and sat next to me.

"Your penis will be swollen. Ice it for twenty minutes on, then twenty minutes off for the rest of the day. Take naproxen the first two days, then switch to ibuprofen until the pain subsides. I will remove the stitches in four to five days.

"I wrapped your penis in sterile gauze. Remove it after twenty-four hours and do not re-bandage it. Wash lightly for the first three days. Empty your bladder frequently to prevent an erection. And that's it. Ralph has my number if you need anything."

"Thanks, Jillie."

"Take care of yourself, Toby."

As she was leaving, I called her. "May I hug you, Jillie?"

She returned and put her arms around me.

"Thanks. My mother should have been here. I can't remember her. I wish I did."

Jillie soothed me, wiping my tears. "I'll be back tomorrow. I have two young men I think you would benefit from meeting, my son River and his husband Cale."

She kissed my cheek and left.

The guys helped me to the couch. I guess I dozed. I woke and the guys asked if I wanted lunch. I thanked them and told them, "Not right now. Just water."

Gabe gave me a pain pill then adjusted my sheet. He kissed my forehead.

"Try to sleep, Toby."

I must have dozed off a second time. I awoke hearing noises in the hall. Clearing my mind, I heard muted voices giving directions. I turned to see men wearing black clothes carrying a body on a stretcher.

"Put him in the first room on the right. Ralph, get Jillie back here, stat."

I rubbed my eyes. "Gabe. What's happening?"

"In a second. Just stay there. Mac, get Toby back on the couch and keep him there. Treat him with kid gloves."

I wanted to ask what kid gloves were. A tall guy dressed in black Ninja clothes with military looking equipment clipped to him was advancing towards me. A humongous gun hugged his hip. That sight frightened me. The man must have seen my eyes.

"Steady kid. I won't hurt you. My name is Mac. I just carry this stuff to keep the good guys safe. You are one of the good guys, right?"

"Yes, I'm a good boy."

"Great. Tell me your name."

"Toby."

"Cool. How old are you Toby?"

"Seventeen."

"That's so cool. I have twins. A boy and a girl. They are seventeen, like you."

"I know what you are trying to do. You want to distract me from what is happening in the bedroom?"

"You are smart for your age, Toby."

I became angry. "Quit patronizing me with your nonsense."

"Okay Toby. I apologize. The boss told me to distract you until he can get over here. He will let you know what's going on soon. Probably after the doc gets here. Why don't you and I hang out here?"

"Do I have a choice?"

"Nope." He smiled. "So, as I told you, my name's Mac. Well, that's what my team calls me. My full name is MacDougall. That's from my Scottish dad."

Before Mac could say more, I saw Jillie hustle through the hall to the other bedroom.

"Who's in that room?" I asked afraid to learn the answer.

"Gabe would be pissed if I told you. We need to wait for him."

Ralph came over to us.

"Thanks Mac."

Sitting on the couch, he asked. "Need a pain pill? Water?

"What's going on? Ralph. Who's in that room?"

"You gotta wait here for Jillie. She will give you a full rundown. Patience, my young Jedi."

I huffed. "Tell me or I'm getting up and you and your men won't stop me."

"Okay." Ralph sighed as if had reached a decision. "Now don't freak. Your brother will be okay. He is in that room."

Mac and Ralph both had to hold me down as I struggled to get to Aiden.

"Aiden!" I hollered, struggling to get off the couch.

"I told you not to freak. You rip those stitches on your penis and Jillie will not be happy."

I forced myself to regain control. "Okay. Just tell me what happened. Why is Aiden hurt?"

Before anyone could say a word, a whirlwind of a kid wearing shorts and a T-shirt raced into the room, followed by a man in black clothing.

"Sorry, Ralph. That little shit is slippery. He got away from me."

"Toby!" Woody flung himself on top of me, kissing me all over.

Ralph and Mac pulled him off. "Careful kid. Your friend is okay. He has stitches. Can't rip them."

"Stitches? What the heck" What happened?"

Next thing, Woody was kneeling next to me, holding my hand.

"Stitches? Tell me about them later. Dude, I thought I lost you. When your brother called and told me your dad had those bastards take you, I lost my mind. I wrecked my room throwing things. ~~Then I started for~~ was running to your house where I see these guys in black, all ninja turtle like smashing in your door. I tried to get at them, but they zip tied me and threw me in some black clown car."

Mac looked put out. "That clown car is an armored SUV."

"Yeah. A clown car." Woody glared at Mac. "Your guys can't zip tie for shit. I was out of them in a New York minute and you guys never caught on."

Mac looked at Ralph and shrugged. "He's a kid. We did not want to hurt him. I have two of my own."

Woody laughed, staring at Mac's black outfit with military looking stuff hanging off it with amusement. "Bet they don't know their daddy is a clown."

I'd heard enough from my friend. "Cool your jet's, boyfriend. These are the good guys. They saved me."

Woody squeaked. "Boyfriend. Oh wow. That's awesome. Let me kiss you."

"Later, Woody. Now tell these nice men you are sorry for dissing them."

"Sorry, guys."

Woody grinned as he said that, so I figured he was only playing at being nice. He sat on the floor, holding my hand.

"Sorry to tell you this, Toby. Your dad's a major dick."

"He is no longer my dad. He is just my sperm donor. He can rot in hell."

Gabe came up in time to hear what I said. "He'll rot all right. By the time the inmates where he is going to finish with him, he'll only wish he was in hell. You do not need to know what they do to abusers of children in our State prisons. He will find out after they find him guilty at his trial. His two buddies are heading to prison with him. We caught them in your house."

"What were they doing in the house?"

My voice sounded small, even to me. Woody squeezed my hand.

Mac took over the narrative. "My team breached the door and found Aiden tied, wearing only his briefs, hanging from hooks, his toes barely touching the floor.

The dad and his two scum buddies held whips ready to use them on Aiden's bare back. He has a couple of red stripes on his back. We believe they were just starting. They had instruments of torture on a nearby table. We subdued the bad guys and tied them. My team suspects they were high on something.

We took pictures of Aiden hanging with his torso's welts visible. The prosecutor needs those for evidence. We called the police. They came and arrested those three. They were not gentle after seeing the torture devices and the ceiling hook from where they suspended Aiden.

We wrapped Aiden in a heated blanket and brought him here."

"I want to see him. Please let me see him. He may need me, please. Woody needs to be with us."

Gabe said. "Give me a minute. I'll see what Jillie says."

Gabe returned. "Woody, you need to help Toby. He has trouble walking."

"I do not." I griped and promptly sagged against Woody as I tried to stand.

Supported by Ralph and Woody, I walked to Aiden's room.

Chapter Four

I could barely see my brother with the tears blurring my eyes. I swiped them allowing my vision to clear, somewhat.

My beautiful baby brother lay on his stomach, with a sheet covering him. Ralph and Woody helped me to sit next to his bed. Aiden turned his head to look at me, his eyes red, his face puffy.

In a soft, yet forceful voice, he said. "I'll be okay, Toby. Dad's too weak to hit me hard. Besides, they were just starting when I got rescued.

Some tough-looking dudes in black Ninja outfits with cool stuff hanging off their clothes busted into the house and surrounded me. I gotta tell you; they impressed me."

Then Aiden lowered his voice. "I learned some super, cool cuss words when they talked about dad and his buddies. Want to hear them?"

"Let's save the teaching of swear words for later." Gabe grinned.

Jillie stood on the other side of Aiden's bed, as Gabe began a summary of another part of the action at the house.

"Aiden is both lucky and a fighter. Lucky because my warriors rescued him before any actual damage to his body happened. He is a fighter because he kicked two of the men with his bare feet so hard one lost a couple of teeth. Those guys had to zip tie his ankles trying to keep him still. The men who breached the door say Aiden was swearing like a drunken United States Marine and kicking as much as he was able. They think his fight slowed their plans."

Aiden snorted. "I had just begun to fight."

Smiling at Aiden, Jillie told Aiden about his injuries.

"Okay, mister tough guy. Let me tell you about your injuries. A few welts from a belt. wrist burns from when you fought back, and do you remember being cut?"

Aiden shook his head.

There is a deep gash across your shoulders. You needed twenty stitches. You sure you never felt a cut?"

"Nope."

"Could have been the adrenaline flowing. Well, I got you stitched, bandaged, and healing. Rest. I'll see you in the morning."

Looking at Gabe, I asked. "Can the three of us sleep in your king-sized bed tonight? I want us to be together. I promise all we will do is sleep."

Gabe chuckled. "Gonna be crowded with the four of us in it."

"Uh, Gabe. you gotta use another bed. We want yours."

Ralph laughed. "You can bunk with me. My beds a queen. That's enough room for the both of us."

"What do you say, Jillie? That okay?"

"Not really. Toby needs help to get to the toilet. Aiden should not walk without someone helping him, either."

Toby looked at Gabe. "Okay, mister watchman. You can shack up with the three of us."

Gabe looked astonished. "Where did you kids learn the term shack up?"

"YouTube." Woody replied with a grin.

"The three of you take the bed. I like the recliner. It's comfortable. I can get up easier and not disturb you guys."

When the time came to sleep, Ralph helped Woody ease Aiden and myself into the bed. Woody made sure we were comfortable before taking the edge of the bed for himself.

GABE Woody told me later what happened *in the morning* after we dozed off.

I left you boys and went to find Jillie to thank her for all she had done before seeing her out the front door. *You entered*

Returning to the living room, I saw *who sat* Pat and Mac on the couch sucking on beers.

"Did either of you get me one of those?" *Toby asked*

"We brought you a can of soda. Ralph pointed to the table next to my chair.

After I sat, Mac began a summary of the take down at the house.

I interrupted. "You have pictures and evidence to send those scum away?"

"Of course, Toby. When we finish our testimony and the police officers finish theirs, no way your dad and his buddies will walk."

"Good," I sighed.

Ralph asked Mac. "What about those two upstairs? Social Services will be investigating. Foster placement probably is their destination."

Mac's face scrunched. "Toby is a month away from turning eighteen. If he has a safe place to live, they will probably wave placement, Ralph."

"Aiden needs to stay with his brother. They have a symbiotic relationship."

"Speak in English, Gabe."

"That means Mac, a relationship exists between these brothers where each depends on and receives reinforcement from the other. ~~For these~~ two, I see this as a benefit. Both have strong, independent personalities, so this relationship probably is not detrimental."

"Smart guy, Mister Legionnaire. The Foreign Legion provide you with an education?"

I saw Gabe's eyes gaze at the White Kepi.

"I keep that Kepi safe on the top shelf of my bookcase. That hat symbolizes my sacrifice and learning. I earned the Kepi as a member of the La Légion étrangère, the French Foreign Legion. And yes, they provided me with an education."

We sit in silence, lost in thought. Mac finished his beer then told us he will see us tomorrow. We tell him to stay safe.

"You know," Ralph looks at Gabe. We could do it. We could do for them what Cian and Jason did for us, how Cian and Jason accepted us into a home filled with men and boys who only saw the good in us.

Thanks to them, we finished high school and you joined the French Foreign Legion.

"Well you know, but for Toby's benefit, I planned to join the United States Marines, just like our older stepbrother Chad, who had served in the Corps. He was my wrestling coach at school. I adored him and so much wanted to be like him.

I chanced upon a YouTube video of the French Foreign Legion, La Légion étrangère. I became fascinated how the Legion went to places where the French Army could not be sent. The Legion was tough and fought wars all over the globe. Those qualities attracted my teen mind.

I changed my plans to become a Marine.

I said goodbye to you guys, hugged Chad hard, thanking him. I traveled to the Legion recruiting office in Paris.

After selection and training, I fought in battles around the world. I finished my five years commitment and accepted a discharge keeping my Legion name given me upon enlistment, Gabriel Martin, and my white kepi, Le Kepi blanc, the hat earned by becoming a Legionnaire.

My past name, Pat Ivanov, died when I entered the Legion. I was no longer the boy who my uncle sold for the use of men. I rose from those ashes to become Gabriel "Gabe" Martin.

Ralph and I formed our company, Étrangere Security. We hired only ex-military personnel trained in special operations. We took the tough jobs no other company felt qualified to tackle. That's about the entire story." *better play*

"Gabe. ~~Gabe. We~~ You ~~need to think~~ how we are going to keep those two from getting shipped off to foster care."

"We better call Cian. He has the connections. Let's use them."

Chapter Five

Cian arrived early the next morning. Over coffee, he listened to Gabe and Ralph explain Toby and Aiden's situation.

"We've got two brothers upstairs whose old man abused them. He is heading to prison. They are heading into the foster care system unless you help us."

Ralph laid the photos, documenting the abuse the brothers suffered in front of Cian.

While he studied the photos, I thought about all the boys and young men he rescued and raised as his own, along with his son Jason, a Hobart police detective.

All boys who came to live with Cian and Jason were functioning adults thanks to the family. Ralph and I were two of these boys rescued and raised by Cian.

He set the pictures on the table as he shook his head, more in sorrow than in anger.

"I can help. Judges dislike separating siblings, especially brothers, unless a compelling reason is present. I can assure you these two will not be separated."

He opened his cell.

"Hi. This is Cian. See if you can get a hearing with Judge Griner for this afternoon. Yes, it's a guardianship hearing."

He handed the cell to me. "Give them the boy's names."

"Hello? Yes. Their names are Toby Matthewson, 17. His brother is Aiden Matthewson, 15. Me? I'm Gabriel Martin. Ralph Ivanov is my brother. We want to be named as co-guardians to the boys."

I returned the cell to Cian.

"Try to get the hearing at Gabriel's house. Both boys cannot travel because of injuries. I need this decided today. Okay. I'll wait."

He covered the cell.

"I think it's better if we get this hearing moved here." He returned his attention to the phone. "One fifteen. Fine, and thanks."

the call

Disconnecting, he said to Ralph and me. "It's a done deal. Now let me meet these two brothers."

In the bedroom, all the boys were ~~awake~~. Woody sat in the chair. Toby and Aiden lay on the bed, a light sheet covering the two brothers.

"I helped them use the toilet. I redressed Toby's penis. I used the ointment."

I smiled. "You are a good friend, Woody."

Looking at two heads peeking up from the sheet, I asked. "You two ~~sleep well?~~ Feeling better?"

Seeing their nods, I introduced them to their lawyer.

"This is Cian Breslin. He is a family law attorney who specializes in guardianship cases. He has arranged for a judge to be here this afternoon. The judge will hold a hearing granting guardianship of the two of you to Ralph and me. If you agree and the judge okays the guardianship, you won't go into foster care. Do each of you want this?"

Toby spoke. His voice full of surprise. "We could live with you and Ralph?" Would you allow Woody to come over, even spend the night?"

"Not a problem, Toby. And you won't have to switch schools, either of you."

Aiden stared for a long time at his brother. Finally, he nodded.

"Okay. Let's do this."

The hearing went as planned. Presented with the pictures and knowing the father was headed for prison, the judge granted temporary guardianship to Ralph and me.

The brothers were now our wards. We rejoiced by eating pizza and drinking soda.

Woody finished his third piece of pizza. Looking at us with a quizzical expression, he asked.

"So you two own a security firm with lots of operatives. You have an attorney on speed dial who knows judges that can bend the law for you. There's a doctor on call. You have a fleet of armored SUV's, that resemble clown cars. You probably have a ton of weapons available."

"You got it all figured out, kid. Well, except for the clown car bit. The armor on that SUV will stop a .50 caliber round. What weapons we use are on a need to know basis, only."

"How you gonna find time to hang with my two buds and give them guidance if you are chasing after bad guys?"

Woody had summed up our situation well. The kid was intuitive, with a hefty dose of snark.

"We thought we'd leave that to you." Ralph replied with a smile.

Gabe spoke up focusing his attention on Woody.

"These two are very important to us. We plan to raise them as our sons and give them loving guidance. You can check on how well we do, Woody, since you can be here as often as your parents permit."

Woody used the two fingers in the eye sign then pointed them at us.

"You better. I'm going to be watching you two."

"We hope you will. If you see us screwing up, call us on it."

Jillie came by to check on the boys and their dressings. They sat on the couch letting her do what she needed. Toby was not even embarrassed, letting us observe his post-op progress. I noticed Woody seemed to look longer at Toby than he did at Aiden.

Jillie gave them her assessment.

"Both Toby and Aiden are healing well. No signs of infection. Aiden's bandages can be removed tomorrow. We'll just leave his shirt off for the next couple of days. Toby, I need to remove your stitches. Try to urinate frequently. If you feel your penis hardening, Ice it. Next week you should be okay."

She did quick work with the stitches while we watched.

"When can we return to school?"

"Aiden can return next week, say Monday. Toby, you should be ready at the end of next week, say Thursday. Okay?"

Toby and Aiden were excited, as was Woody. I could see the smiles all the way to their eyes.

Woody plopped onto the couch close to Toby.

"Not too close, Woody. Your nearness may cause a reaction in a certain body part that needs to be left alone."

"Hey, Aiden. Get your brother ice. He needs to be take care."

Toby shoved Woody's shoulder.

"Jerk."

Then Toby turned serious. "I don't think I'm gay, Woody. Boys don't interest me when I look at them. I might be demisexual."

"What's that mean?"

Toby smiled and reached for Woody's hand.

"It means doofus. I only feel sexual attraction to you, and only you. I'm sure I am attracted to you. Plus, I like looking at you wearing your makeup."

I miss having my kit. But then something about you, your caring heart, how we have engaging talks attracts me...."

"You have said nothing about my cute face and toned body."

"Well, you've got those."

"Be right back." Woody raced to the spare room. He returned, his feet slapping the floor. He slid to a stop in front of Toby, a bag in his hands.

Toby's eyes widened and fille with tears when he saw the package Woody held.

"How did you find my makeup kit?" He asked reaching for it.

"I saw it on the kitchen table after they rescued Aiden and I could enter the house. I grabbed it. With everything going on, I forgot it until now."

Woody handed the kit bag to Toby, who took it with shaking hands.

"Thank you, Woody."

Toby patted the couch, indicating Woody needed to sit next to him.

Toby held the bag to his chest with his left hand. The right hand he put over Woody's shoulders. Pulling Woody to him so their lips were inches apart, his eyes sought permission.

Woody nodded, his face reddened, then leaned in to brush Toby's lips.

"You mean a lot to me. Thank you." Toby told his friend as their lips parted.

Woody placed his hand on Toby's forearm leaning against his friend.

Ralph and Gabe entered the room. "You need ice, Toby?"

The boys looked at these two strong men who wanted to help them be what their hearts told them they could be with a deep love, a love unlike anything they had felt before.

"We have a lot to thank you for."
Toby said as he patted Woody's hand.

"Remember what Jillie said,"
The boys went to their room.

"Sleep well, you three." Gabe and
Ralph said from the doorway.

Tony lay curled against Woody, who
lay on his back. Both of us snuggled close.

Aiden patted my arm. I felt he was
permitting me to share my love for him with
Woody.

In the days that followed, the boys
contented themselves with affectionate
touches and signs of caring. Their love for
each other deepened as the weeks passed.
Woody became closer with both boys,
sharing his love with them.

Gabe and Ralph smiled as Aiden and
Toby recovered and at the growing
attraction between the three boys.

The End

Thanks for reading this story.
My other books are available at Amazon.com
Search Art Gibson Finding Family
Thanks: *Art*
Contact me at <u>acgib1943@protonmail.com</u>

<u>Finding Family Series</u>
Finding Family Crispin and Dylan
Finding Family Ash
Finding Family Mike and Billy
Finding Family College Life

<u>The Ironton Boys Series</u>
Four For All
Saving Timmy
Ironton Boys

<u>Stand Alones</u>
Lead Me On Caleb and Bobby
After We Became Brothers
Coming Together
<u>Paranormal Short Stories</u>
My Twin Died: Then He Returned
The Basement Door

LGBTQ bullying, Human trafficking, and Systemic Racism exist

In my research, I learned how pervasive these issues are in the United States and the World. Though this story is for adults, some behaviors I researched so vile that I chose not to include them in a story teens might read.

This story and other of my stories show that love and understanding exist within caring individuals. Hope exists.

The Trevor Project

The Trevor Project is a national organization providing crisis intervention and suicide prevention services to lesbian, gay, bisexual, transgender, queer, and questioning young people under twenty-five.

If you are a parent of a gay, bisexual, lesbian, or transgender teen, love them. Know that rejecting your teen during this vulnerable time of their life can cause a suicide attempt. Teens whose families reject them are eight times more likely to attempt suicide than youth from families who accept them as they are, according to the Trevor Project.

A discredited practice known as conversion therapy has the same statistics for youth suicide because of its negative effects on the teen.

The *Trevor Project* provides 24/7 crisis support services to LGBTQ young people.

Text, chat, or call anytime to reach a trained counselor. 1-866-488-7386

or at thetrevorproject.org

Made in the USA
Coppell, TX
19 November 2024